Advance Praise

Refreshing challenges to the stereotypes about men that linger in our society. Jonathon brings out the strengths, the distinctions and the humanity of men that reminds us how the sexes can complement and enhance one another. He takes every hot spot in dating and shines a light making sense of the motivations of men that often leave women mystified. Here is a guide, a reference, packed with jewels that women may return to many times over in order to gain an honest perspective about the commitment patterns of the opposite sex. Thank you for your contribution, Jonathon!

~ Greta Hassel, MFT, Intimacy Coach and Sexual Educator

I was definitely enlightened by the male perspective. Unfortunately, this information often came to me (at the age of 57) after many challenging relationships. Ideally, it's something that we should learn about before the dating process begins. I am a firm believer in early education. While the fundamentals of education are important, it's also important for young people learn about practical life skills...which ultimately includes dating and relationships. Take it on the road, Jonathan...start teaching younger generations now...so that they have a better understanding of how to handle such sensitive situations.

~ Anne

Jonathon is a fabulous relationship coach and confidant. He is a decoder ring for the male dating mind. It is so important as women that we are clean in our intentions, communication and expectations. This book starts the conversation in navigating the dynamics of male and female communication. Thank you for this resource, Jonathon. You are a gem.   ~ Teffie

I purchased this book to see exactly how other relationship "experts" depict the forces that lead men to commit in relationships and stay committed. I was pleasantly surprised to see how well the author hits the nail on its head. His description of men as hunters, and discussion of the various factors that keep some men happily content at home, while others continue to hunt new game was particularly insightful. I recommend this book to anyone wanting to understand the male mind and masculine patterns in relationship.   ~ D. Cohen

UNDERSTAND

MEN

NOW

UNDERSTAND

MEN

NOW

the relationships men commit to and why

By Jonathon Aslay

Disclaimer

The information provided in this book is designed to be intellectually and conversationally stimulating, and for enlightenment purposes only. It is not intended to replace the advice and care of your physician, nor is it intended to be used for mental or medical diagnosis & treatment. Jonathon Aslay makes no guarantees or any representations that he will find you a match or resolve your relationship issue - his ideas are merely designed to help you make a shift in a positive direction.

Dedicated to all women in their mid-life

who are single and want to be

part of a couple;

who would like to

to break through

the darkness

and reach

clarity in dating, mating,

and relating.

TABLE OF CONTENTS

AUTHOR'S NOTE

MY NAME IS JONATHON ASLAY - I AM A MID- LIFE DATING AND RELATIONSHIP EXPERT, A SPEAKER, A COACH, AND THE AUTHOR OF *ONLINE DATING SECRETS REVEALED*.

I SPECIALIZE IN DEFENDING AND PROTECTING WOMEN'S HEARTS IN THE EVER-EVOLVING AND OFTEN CONFUSING WORLD OF RELATIONSHIPS - WHETHER THAT BE THE SEARCH FOR A RELATIONSHIP, THE PROGRESSION OF A RELATIONSHIP OR EVEN THE DEMISE OF A RELATIONSHIP IN ORDER THAT WOMEN FIND AND ENJOY THE BEST TYPE OF RELATIONSHIP FOR THEM.

I SOMETIMES CALL MYSELF THE GUY SPY - BUT IN REALITY I AM A KIND OF DOUBLE AGENT - I UNDERSTAND HOW A SINGLE OR DIVORCED MAN THINKS AND I USE THIS KNOWLEDGE TO ASSIST WOMEN IN UNDERSTANDING MEN AS WELL. THE UPSIDE TO THIS IS THAT THE MEN WHO ARE INVOLVED WITH THE WOMEN I TEACH GET TO ENJOY A WOMAN WHO UNDERSTANDS THEM TOO, AND AS WITH ANY DEAL, IT SHOULD BE FAIR AND EQUAL TO ALL PARTIES

INVOLVED - I GET THE SATISFACTION OF HELPING WOMEN UNDERSTAND MEN SO THAT MEN AND WOMEN ARE BOTH HAPPY. PERFECT!

I AM WELL AWARE THAT EVERY RELATIONSHIP IS A TWO WAY STREET, AND I FULLY UNDERSTAND THAT A WOMAN WANTS TO FIND A MAN WHO CARES FOR HER, RESPECTS HER, CHERISHES AND ADORES HER - AS SHE SHOULD... AND SO, I HAVE WRITTEN *UNDERSTAND MEN NOW* AS A SIMPLE, CLEAR AND EASY TO READ GUIDE FOR WOMEN TO FIND THE MAN THAT IS RIGHT FOR THEM, NOT ONLY FOR THE PRESENT BUT ALSO FOR THE FUTURE.

I HOPE MY INSIGHTS, IDEAS, SUGGESTIONS AND OFFERINGS WILL HELP YOU *UNDERSTAND MEN NOW* AND FIND A MAN WHO SUITS YOU, ENHANCES YOUR LIFE AND GIVES YOU THE LOVE THAT YOU DESIRE AND DESERVE.

This book is designed to simplify the complicated and clarify the confusing so that you **can...**

UNDERSTAND MEN
NOW!

INTRODUCTION
* some points to note

i am here to assist you in finding and maintaining a great love with a man who is deserving of you and appreciative of your place in his life.

there are some truths, some facts, some factors and some ideas that i want to share with you in order that your search *for* love and your success *in* love is easier than it might otherwise have been.

the knowledge i share will always come from a place of goodness and strength and will always be given without condition.

i have to assume you are aware that every relationship requires a consistent amount of effort on your part - the knowledge you glean from this book will assist you in understanding how to be in a loving, long-term relationship with a man that is a worthwhile investment of your time, your love, even your life.

in this book i am trying to make my points as succinctly as i can - i will not labor the point, but i will make the point, and if that point seems to be made in a way that you find too strong or too powerful, i apologize, it is just that some points cannot be avoided and are best made in the clear light of day, not shrouded in a convenient soft focus that only blurs the message. i will not enter the religious debate in any way because i believe that all religion is based around one thing - love - and I also do not believe in interfering in your personal beliefs too much.

this book is not about what men are **not** giving you, this book is about helping you to UNDERSTAND MEN NOW - if you feel that you are doing all the work in your relationship, if you feel neglected or taken for granted, then you are in the wrong relationship with the wrong man - this book is here to work in your favor, to help you find a man who is right for you.

i am not advocating that you can change a man, i am simply assisting you in finding *your* right man by understanding how men work - in this way, you can find the best **in** him so that he is the best **for** *you*.

WE ALL WANT
TO BE **LOVED**

We all want to be LOVED. Men, women, boys, girls... even superheroes. Without LOVE we do not feel connected in a way that matters. Without LOVE we are left to feel destitute, lonely, vulnerable, even angry. This holds true for both WOMEN *and* MEN. Yes, men want LOVE too...- Men want to give and receive LOVE... Men want what women want - *a connection that has meaning.*

The more we understand that men and women are both seeking the same outcome in their relationships, the more chance we have of succeeding together, as a team, in unison, successful, and happy.

My quest is to help women
UNDERSTAND MEN NOW –
and I want to start with a simple observation:

If humans thrive on LOVE, then it holds true that both women and men want LOVE, which means that men and women have the same goals, the same dreams, the same desires and the same wishes. I would like you to be clear that men and women are on common ground as humans, as partners, as LOVERS - it is just the communication and understanding that confuses us...

MEN

Allow me to start by making an observation about
MEN:
Most MEN are really just 21 years old...

Even if a man in is in his 40's, 50's or 60's, he still thinks like a 21 year old, he still harps back to the good old days, he still has the same conversations with his friends about sports, cars, girls.

A man might be world —educated, not college educated...

He might be married, divorced or still a bachelor...

He might be book smart not street smart...

He might be blue collar or white collar...

He might be perfectly imperfect...

Whatever a man has been
does not necessarily determine where he will go

You see, there is no *ticking clock* for a man, there is no *time line* for him to start a family, there is no *pressure* to grow up, to be mature, to be an adult. MEN have the luxury of time... and that translates into MEN holding on to their youth.

Some men play the field and never stop.
Others marry young and divorce quickly.
*Most men are looking for that **perfect love** - they might never have been married, they might be divorced.*

I am often told by women that they are not interested in a man who has not been married by the time he is 40 - this man is persona non grata...which means she might have just *missed* **a great guy.** Perhaps he was **very sure** of what he was looking for in the woman he wants to be with and has not found it (until he met you); perhaps he has had some **long term loves** but they did not want marriage (even though he did); perhaps he wanted to **live a little** before he made such a serious commitment (but now he is older and has played the field); perhaps only now is he ready for marriage - perfect timing for you!

I always try to encourage women to at least give a man a chance - he might not be right for you, but he might have a friend for you... He might be totally wrong for you, but at least you have gained experience...

Of course, there are those men that have never been married for good reason - he could be an eternal player, he might not be set up for the long term relationship (instead opting for the short term alliances), he may even be peculiar (and so nobody could handle it!)

There are 2 sides to every story - so look at each man with fresh eyes - ***do not judge him on his past*** - judge him on his behavior with you...As for the man that has been married and divorced by the time he is 40 - this man has his 2 sides as well.

Perhaps he has shown that a **commitment** is important to him; perhaps he married the wrong girl first time around and has **learned from his mistake**; perhaps marriage helped him become a **real man**; perhaps his children are grown and he is now **ripe for a great relationship**, and a great **marriage**...

On the other side of this coin is the fact that he made a lifelong promise and did not keep it (which might not bother you if you are a divorcee as well), or maybe he decided that marriage was too much of a commitment and he never wants to do it again, he might have been badly burned by his Ex and now is once bitten twice shy and therefore should be avoided because he is either angry or scared.

Again, ***do not judge him on his past*** - judge him on his behavior with you...

If a man has been married and divorced...

he might now be enjoying his freedom

If a man has never been married...

he might now be ready to settle down

"Consider how hard it is to change yourself and you'll understand what little chance you have in trying to change others"

MEN ARE <u>NOT</u> COMMITMENT PHOBIC

No matter what you have been told, or what may be convenient reasoning, **men are not commitment phobic** - in fact, I would argue that they are the complete opposite - why else would they keep spending inordinate amounts of time, effort and money on trying to find themselves something meaningful?

Granted, there are many men out there who want to be in love, who want to be in a great relationship, who want to build a life with a woman, but who do not seem capable of *communicating*, *understanding* or *maintaining* a meaningful relationship - this does not mean they are a lost cause, it means they are a treasure waiting to be found by the right woman.

The man that does not know *how* to commit is just not the type of man you should be with at the moment - he might have been 'designed' for someone else, or he might not be ready for a full on relationship... yet.

Either way, there will come a time when the right set of circumstances will arise, and that man, the seemingly 'non-committal' male, will fall head over heels into a relationship and a deep, long term love.

There are men who do not appear to know how to commit... but that does not mean they do not want to commit...

Men do not need to be forced into a commitment - they will make it **very clear when they want it** and they will be **very unclear when they do not** - listen to what they say, watch how they behave and take note of the signals they send.

Trying to force a man into a commitment will send him in the wrong direction, allow him to think it is his idea and he will be ALL yours.

Although there are many generalized opinions on the male of the species, and even though these may be convenient excuses as to why a man will not commit, I am a firm believer that **men _do_ want to be involved in a great love**, just as women do - you see, the human in us is not that different, it is just that men and women go about their search in different ways, and this is where the confusion sets in, the communication breaks down, and the relationship comes to an end.

I am a HOPEFUL ROMANTIC and so I am going to give you simple and workable ideas that will **clear up** the misconceptions and offer up **solutions** to the age old dating problems that women have faced - problems that are nobody's fault in particular, but problems that have caused numerous obstacles to men and women finding a lasting and great love.

If you can move forward in the understanding that _men are not commitment phobic_, then you open up a myriad of opportunities to succeed in love, and just as women look for love, men are available for love; take off the armor, open up your hearts and see what you can discern from my unique and shockingly simple insight that will not only give you the tools and the answers you seek, but will help you understand...what men want in a relationship.

"Any woman can fool a man if she wants to and if he's in love with her"

julie hintz

WHAT MEN WANT IN A RELATIONSHIP

One of the most confusing aspects of relationships is the perception that men and women want something different from a relationship - that men want a woman who stays at home and women want a man who gathers and provides.

This may have been true in times gone by, but now we have a whole new playing field to contend with - we live longer.

we have more options and possibilities.

we find women who love their work and men who love their family more than their work.

we have **role reversal, role inclusion, gender confusion** and a world where women are capable of being far more particular in their choice of partner - all of which should be seen as a great **opportunity to enjoy that one special love.**

With equality becoming more commonplace in life and

in love, men are left a little confused - what they have been taught and what they have to deal with are very different, and because of this, their behavior might not always be easy to contend with for women - but rest assured, this is no deliberate ploy on the part of men, it is simply a 'growing phase' that men will overcome!

Women now have a great opportunity to find the exact criteria they are looking for **without need or desperation, without fear or confusion** - as the lines between male and female roles become more blurred, men are finding that what women want out of a relationship is the same as what they want -

love, companionship,
equality & trust

Because of the shift in the equation, men can allow women to have a sense of *self achievement* without feeling threatened.

Because of the shift in ideals, men are able to *support* the women they love without fear of inferiority.

Because of the shift in outlook, men are *encouraged* to be a loving, caring and rounded individual, which plays into the fact that men AND women want to build a solid foundation to their relationship - men want to grow with the woman they love and admire, men want to encourage their love *and* be encouraged by their love.

As the old roles are slowly but surely erased, the emerging roles of men and women pose new challenges, yes, but they also pose better opportunities for men to be **loving, caring** *and* **supportive**

... *which is, in* fact
what men really want in a relationship.

"You make me want to be a better man"
as good as it gets

HOW & WHY MEN
FALL IN LOVE

Although men love to be in love, they do not walk around looking for love in the same way a woman might...

Men are a little **frightened** by love
     whereas women are usually **overjoyed** by it

Men are a little **confused** by love
     whereas women often **glow** because of it

For a man, love is often perceived as a responsibility - perhaps it is the teachings of the past, or the knight in shining armor stories that have men thinking that love is something they 'take on' rather than something they can enjoy...

But this does not stop men from falling in love often... and powerfully.

In fact, it appears that men cannot help themselves... _HOW and WHY men fall in love_ is not terribly complicated, and in fact it is essentially about the woman allowing the man to be a man, to be the protective male, to be her romantic mate - which is actually exactly what a rounded and balanced woman should want...

Men fall in love because they are made to feel like men. How that happens is not a mystery... Men are **HUNTERS** - plain and simple.

fact - if the hunt ends, men give up

Therefore, it is a wise idea to keep a man *hunting*.

How?

By not always being available. Once in a while, be unavailable for plans he might want to make - in this way you maintain the mystery which prolongs the desire for him to hunt, and keeps his desire heightened.

By changing up your appearance. It pays off to look foxy one day, relaxed the next, wear your hair up on a weekend and down at a social event in this way you demonstrate many facets to your appearance and he will equate that to your personality because men are visual beings which will keep him interested.

By making sure you have things to do. Make sure to maintain outside friendships, have your own interests and forge your own plans - in this way you show that you are a catch, a go-getter, an active and desirable woman who does not need him all the time.

By always allowing him to be the man. Let him make decisions and take control when you can - in this way, he will feel like a man and his libido will rise because you are his fair maiden.

Men are also **PROTECTORS**.

If a man feels useless
                    he will stop being a good partner

Therefore it is wise to keep a man active as a *protector*.

How?

By asking his opinion on things that matter to you.
Asking a man for his opinion makes him feel like his thoughts matter to you - practical or emotional matters, men want to feel that their ideas count with the woman they are attracted to.

By wearing soft clothes that make you feel fragile to him. Men have a subconscious chemical reaction to soft fabrics and materials - by wearing delicate clothing, a woman encourages a protection mechanism in her man... and that's a good thing for both parties!

By giving him jobs that make him feel manly and capable. From changing a lightbulb to carrying something for you, a man wants to feel that he is invaluable - if you give him the opportunity to do something for you, you will trigger his desire to protect you even more.

By showing him that you need his strength. There are times when you will genuinely need him to protect you, when his strength is indispensable to your life - if you choose these times wisely and allow him to 'man up' to the occasion, you will embolden his desire and strengthen your love.

The above points are NOT designed as ways to play a game with a man's heart, they are designed to keep you and your man on an equal and exciting footing because you are now a mysterious, rounded and balanced woman who values his masculinity, his strength, his input, his existence in your life - if you can encourage a man to be a man, if you show gratitude for his manliness, if you appreciate his manly qualities, you come across as the woman who **chooses** him to be in your life, not because you need him, but because you want him - which is sexy for you... and for him.

"Look, I guarantee there'll be tough times. I guarantee that at some time, one or both of us is gonna want to get out of this thing. But I also guarantee that if I don't ask you to be mine, I'll regret it for the rest of my life, because I know, in my heart, you're the only one for me"

runaway bride

TYPES OF (AVAILABLE) MEN

Basically, there are 2 TYPES OF MEN available to women.

The guy who has NEVER been married.

The man who is NO LONGER married.

There is the SINGLE guy *with* kids and the SINGLE guy *without*, the SINGLE guy who no longer sees his kids and the SINGLE guy who is solely responsible for those kids.

There is the DIVORCED man with kids that he rarely sees, the DIVORCED man who is an extremely active parent, the WIDOWER who has small children and the WIDOWER whose children have left home.

** One would hope that a man with children would still be an active, loving and committed parent - however, with the law courts promising fairness but not always achieving justice there are numerous variations that could cause a man to be estranged from his children to some degree or other - what matters is that he **wants** to*

be an active parent, that he demonstrates this, and that he makes an effort to be one (in whatever capacity he can).

A man who disregards his children
is not a man to be involved with

As a woman looking to UNDERSTAND MEN NOW, it is imperative that you allow your **gut instinct** to play a part in your choice of partner.

Your **gut instinct** never lies
it is designed to **protect** you

You will know whether a man is truly nurturing or simply posturing by the way you feel when you are around him, and you will see from the way he behaves with you whether he is a man who stands by the courage of his convictions.

The man you want does not necessarily have to be single, or have to have been married - the man you want is someone whose words & actions go together, a man who makes you feel secure, a man who has your best interests at heart, a man who speaks his truth and lives that truth...

It does not matter what a man has done or has not done, providing he has done 2 things:

-Learned from his mistakes.

-Learned to live with honesty and integrity.

The SINGLE guy who has reached (or even passed) his forties is not necessarily a lost cause - he might have been wise enough to wait until he was sure of himself before he decided to fully commit to a lifelong love.

The DIVORCED man might have learned from his mistake and might have opened up into a far more mature male from the experience. All in all, whatever a guy (or a man) is or is not at this time does not necessarily dictate how he will be in a committed relationship - perhaps the SINGLE guy was a faithful and loving partner to 3 or more long term loves... or the DIVORCED man married his first love and needs more experience - the **possibilities** are endless, and the **opportunities** are available. It is not his past that matters, it is his present, his presence, his persistence and his ability to be prepared to commit when it truly matters. There is a multitude of men out there - all of whom are suited to a different woman in some way or other.

UNDERSTAND **MEN NOW** is your way to finding the right man that fits *your* personality, *your* desires, *your* wants, wishes, goals and dreams.

Do not make assumptions based on the past - listen to your **gut instinct**, learn from *your* mistakes and allow him to demonstrate what *TYPE OF MAN* he can be for YOU. Once you have got past the initial stereo-typical thoughts about a particular situation, you can then make an assessment and a judgment on the actual person you are with - men are simple creatures in many ways but they are not always easy to understand from a woman's point of view - they do have their upside, and that is what we aim to find for you.

* as a side note here, I would like to talk briefly about the DIVORCED MAN WITH CHILDREN - for this man might have a dilemma if he is to date a woman with children - and here is his dilemma: if he decides to date a woman who has children, and if that relationship evolves into something deep and meaningful, will he be neglecting his own children whilst nurturing someone else's children? Will he be choosing to spend time **without** *his kids in return for spending time* **with** *the woman he loves (and her kids)?*

i know that every case is different depending on his relationship with his children, his relationship with his Ex, who has custody, the age of his children, the ability to include his children in his girlfriend's life etc... but I do want to point out that the DIVORCED MAN WITH CHILDREN may have to deal with this dilemma, this adjustment in his life, and this might be because he wants to be a great father (as well as being a great partner to you) - if this dilemma arises, it comes from a place of good, of strength, of responsibility... and should be dealt with accordingly... with **love***.*

MEN & CHILDREN

There is a prevailing belief in society that a woman who is divorced with children (or a single mother) is someone that men will actively avoid because she comes with 'baggage'.

Not so.

I know of many men that actually WANT a woman who has children.

This could be for a number of reasons:

-He may find her maternal instinct intoxicating because he admires his own mother.

-He might want a woman whom he knows has other responsibilities so they have guaranteed space in their relationship.

-He might enjoy spending time with children but does not want his own because of numerous reasons (time constraints, travel for work, financial responsibility, emotional responsibility).

- He might not be able to have children.

- He might have lost a child earlier in his life.

- He might even have tried and failed in a previous relationship.

Whatever his reasons might be, there are plenty of men that will deliberately choose a 'single mother' because it suits their lifestyle, it fills an emotional void, it allows them to be a positive influence on a child without having to be totally available or fully responsible for that child's entire existence. I mention this type of man because I want **divorced** mothers, **widowed** mothers and **single** mothers to know that NOT all men view a child or children as 'baggage' - many men view children as a bonus and a privilege, and these men are the type of man you should be dating because

- these men truly understand *and* value the importance of motherhood.

- these men view motherhood as sexy.

- these men will not give you ultimatums when it comes to your children and the priority that children naturally hold in your life.

May it now prevail through your life that a mother-with-children is not always viewed as a woman-with-baggage, that she has every right, every chance and every opportunity to find a great guy who wants to assist in nurturing and enjoying her children whilst loving her fully and properly.

A LITTLE TRICK WITH MEN

Men love to be _loved_.

Men like to be **encouraged**.

Men want to be **appreciated**.

A LITTLE TRICK WITH MEN ...

is to offer them **_encouragement..._**
and then to show **_appreciation._**

Encouragement can come in many guises - it might be *encouraging* him to be a man and do a chore; it could be *encouraging* him to take a risk with a new and viable business; it might be **encouragement** of an emotional kind - whatever a woman can do to *encourage* a man to feel that he *CAN*, will work in her favor and in the favor of the relationship.

If a woman is full of **encouragement** for her man she will inspire him to be better, to be there, to be greater than he ever thought he could be - not only for himself, but also for his woman, his love, his biggest fan.
If that **encouragement** is backed up with **appreciation**, then the woman will find herself with a *dedicated* man who wants to demonstrate and impress his love upon her in every way he can.

Appreciation may be shown through private words, by cooking in the kitchen, with actions in the bedroom, or by moments of public affection - if the appreciation is doled out willingly and often, a woman will find herself adored, respected and content because she will have a man who wants to be everything he can be... for her.

That's *A LITTLE TRICK WITH MEN*
TELL HIM WHAT YOU WANT

Men are generally happy that *women* are *women*.

Men know that women are more expressive, more

emotional, more communicative...

Men even understand that they have been brought up to hide their emotions, to be strong, to be braver than women (and other men).

Men want to do the right thing for their woman... and they want to still be a man...

Even if a man does not fully understand **how** a woman works, he will more often than not try to please a woman he loves by doing what he perceives to be the right thing...

sometimes he gets it right

sometimes he does not

If a man makes the effort and he does not get it right, then it is in a woman's best interest to **tell him what she wants** -

but do it from a place of love...

be aware of his ego...

do it gently...

Men respond better to being **told** what you want than they do to being berated for making the effort and getting it wrong...

Whatever it is that you want, **ask** for it clearly - do not demand it or manipulate him for it.

And the way to get the **best** out of a man - make him think, feel and realize that it will make *you* happy... then he will see it as an honor, not as a chore.

Once he has done what you asked for, once he has made the effort to please you, the next thing to do is show him that you **appreciate** him for caring about you, for loving you, for doing what you asked him to do...

Then it will be easier the next time because he will know it gives you pleasure... and as I said before, men *want* to make their women happy and pleased.

- **ask** and you shall receive -

"Men are like trains. They are going somewhere. Choosing and staying with a man is like choosing to get on a train. You will end up going where your man goes, spiritually and sexually, or you will have to get off his train. You cannot change a man's direction to yours without losing trust in his capacity to navigate"

david deida

THE PRICE
Of the Whole Package

We all know that nothing comes for FREE...

even if we wish it would.

Be prepared to accept certain things about a MAN that I call *THE **PRICE** OF THE WHOLE PACKAGE.*

And rest assured, there are things about YOU that he will have to accept as well - you see... *THE **PRICE** OF THE WHOLE PACKAGE*

*Nobody is **perfect** - sorry... it's just a **FACT***

The **expense** of THE WHOLE PACKAGE is up to you ...

- it might be that you are not prepared to pay much towards this PACKAGE, in which case your boundaries will be tight and rigid and your field of opportunity will be smaller...

- it might be that you are willing to pay more for this

PACKAGE, in which case you will have more choices - but they might not all be pleasant.

When a package arrives on your doorstep it might be wrapped in brown paper, there may be unsightly stamp marks on it, it might even be a bit beaten up from the journey... but you pick it up and you open it - you ordered it after all - and then, under the brown paper and the rough exterior you find a nice new box, and after a deep breath you open that box and you find... exactly what you were looking for.

That is THE PRICE OF THE WHOLE PACKAGE:

You paid for it.

You waited for it.

You finally received it.

You excitedly unwrapped it.

& you found whatever it was you ordered.

Now, I am not suggesting that beneath every male exterior is your perfect interior, but what I am saying is this - NOTHING YOU WANT COMES FOR FREE. _There is always a price to pay..._

From the smallest (and mostly reversible) things, like eating with his mouth open, or dropping his towels on the floor...Through to fundamental (and probably irreversible) issues, such as a filthy temper and poor taste in furniture...*there is always a price to pay for the enjoyment of another.*

What you are prepared to *pay* *is up to you -*

- I would hope that you are not overly critical, or overtly accepting...

- I would hope that you know the difference between a small problem and a major issue...

- I would hope that you can find a balance...so that the price makes the package worthwhile...

Everything has a price ...

be it emotional or financial- Only you can be the judge of what you are willing to pay.

- *The nice men are ugly.*
- *The handsome men are not nice.*
- *The handsome and nice men are gay.*
- *The handsome, nice and heterosexual men are married.*
- *The men who are not so handsome, but are nice men, have no money.*
- *The men who are not so handsome, but are nice men with money think we are only after their money.*
- *The handsome men without money are after our money.*
- *The handsome men, who are not so nice and somewhat heterosexual, don't think we are beautiful enough.*
- *The men who think we are beautiful, that are heterosexual, somewhat nice and have money, are cowards.*
- *The men who are somewhat handsome, somewhat nice and have some money and thank, heaven, are heterosexual, are shy and NEVER MAKE THE FIRST MOVE!!!!*
- *The men who never make the first move, automatically lose interest in us when we take the initiative.*

* See references

MEN & SPACE

MEN are not always the most communicative species on the planet - that bonus gift was given to women...

And sometimes, this causes issues in a relationship - especially at the beginning.

The woman might be overly communicative and the man might see this as pressurizing, although she is only trying to 'keep in touch' or 'demonstrate that she cares'.

MEN need their SPACE - and they need to feel that you need yours... This goes back to the *hunting* scenario.

- If a man feels that a woman is a little **unavailable**, then he will be more inclined to chase her.

- If a man thinks that she has **other options** in her life (men or activities) then he will be more inclined to want her.

- If a man sees that she **does not need** to 'touch base' all the time then he will be more inclined to wonder where she is and what she is doing.
- If you give a man his SPACE - and you make sure to fill

that time with your own projects, trips, friends and life then you will appear to be a 'catch'.

Having said this, it is important not to turn this into a game of avoidance or aloofness - if he does reach out, and you like him, then make sure that you reach back to give him the **encouragement** he needs to keep on chasing you.

"When men attempt bold gestures, generally it's considered romantic. When women do it, it's often considered desperate or psycho."

sex & the city

THE LOVE PIE

In order for you to peak your man's interest, it is advisable to always give him the opportunity to chase you. Men love the chase, and women do not understand what happens when they give in to that chase... and the man walks away.

Why would he do that?

Because he feels as if the fun has left the relationship.

My advice - only ever give **49%**

Do not give 50%. Or even 60... Stop at **49%**

Let *him* carry the other **51%** of the relationship.

In this way you will encourage him to always chase you because he is more invested than you are, he is having to constantly prove that he is worth your time and your love, he is the one who has to walk *towards* you.

For whatever reason, men often give up on their women when they perceive them to be 'too easy' - whether that be a one-night-stand easy or waiting-at-home easy, men do not want to feel that they got something for nothing... or nothing for everything they have.

Men want a fair trade -or at least they want to work towards a fair trade.

If you can **hold yourself back** a little; if you can be **slightly elusive**: if you can **maintain the mystery**: if you can be **patient**, then a man will always *want* you, he will always *chase* you, and he will always *love* you for being able to survive without him.

When it comes to THE LOVE PIE there is a great deal to be gained for the relationship as a whole by the woman maintaining the sexual and emotional tension - this is done with patience.

By patiently allowing him to come to her.

By patiently accepting him for who he is.

By patiently working at only giving **49%**

In the case of THE LOVE PIE, patience is most definitely a virtue that keeps both partners interested **and** excited.

"It is better for a girl to sleep a hundred years and be kissed and awakened by the right prince than to stay awake and be kissed a hundred times by the wrong frog"
                                                    j. johnson

practice PATIENCE

PATIENCE - *the state of endurance **and calm** under difficult circumstances, which can mean persevering in the face of delay or provocation without acting on annoyance/anger in a negative way; or exhibiting forbearance when under strain, especially when faced with longer-term difficulties.*

When it comes to dating, PATIENCE is not only a virtue... it is **invaluable**.

The ability to display PATIENCE has a multi-fold benefit to your dating and loving experience:

- If you have PATIENCE you will create a better relationship.

- If you have PATIENCE you will have an air of confidence.

- If you have PATIENCE you will make wise decisions.

- If you have PATIENCE you will inspire desire.

PATIENCE gives you the chance to really understand what it is you want from a relationship.

PATIENCE gives you the ability to really know who you are dating and loving.

PATIENCE gives you the time to really make sure that you are with the right person for _you_.

* if you do **not** display and practice PATIENCE when it comes to love...

* if you have an agenda and a time frame...

* if you are manipulative and controlling...

you will only ever come across as **weak**, **needy** and **desperate**.

Weakness, neediness and desperation are not your friends - they are your enemies - they are the anti-heroes of **true love** - they are the reason that you make ill-advised decisions that come back to haunt you - they try to force a situation to be something it is **not** - they are the opposite of PATIENCE.

Patience is your friend...

If you display **im**PATIENCE, you are likely to display irritation which means you are going to drive a man away... and at the same time you will drive yourself crazy.

---

*Never run after a **bus** or a **man***

     There will always be another one

As discussed in THE LOVE PIE it is a good idea to always hold back a little, to maintain an air of mystery, to allow a man to **feel** that he has to earn your love and then he will **want** to earn your love, to let him continually work towards a goal that he is never quite sure of achieving...

For example - when you receive a text - practice PATIENCE and do not respond instantly...when you send a text - practice PATIENCE and do not expect a response instantly...

DO NOT make assumptions about his behavior and then jump to conclusions - he might be busy, he might be a slow responder, he might **not** be that into you...

Either way, practice PATIENCE - observe your gut instinct, listen to his words, watch his actions and then you will see the truth because you did not rush into a decision or a drama that may or may not be to your benefit. And this is where PATIENCE is so important -

PATIENCE is the ingredient of a relationship that

encourages you *and* your man to take the time required to nourish the love you both want. Love is a never-ending journey that requires constant nurturing... and PATIENCE is an ingredient that allows you to see your relationship with clarity, to endure the hard times with positivity, and to enjoy the good times with consistency. PATIENCE *IS* a virtue.

GIVE YOUR **RELATIONSHIP**
The Greatest Chance of Success

THE 5 **C**'s

The **5 C**'s are the fundamental building block for any successful, long term, healthy and happy relationship -

If you miss even *one* of these **5 C**'s then your rate of success and happiness in a relationship will be diminished.

THE 5 **C**'s:

chemistry
communication
compatibility
character
continuity
... leading to ***commitment***

chemistry

CHEMISTRY is something you cannot necessarily explain... or define. But that does not make it any less potent or varied - be it physical, emotional, intellectual, creative, philosophical or protective CHEMISTRY.

Without this illusive and exciting CHEMISTRY, we are left with a simple friendship, not a highly charged *connection* - CHEMISTRY is the one element of a relationship that bonds us together like glue, that combines physical attraction with emotional desire, that has us topsy turvy, happy and excited all at once.

Oxytocin bonds a *mother* to her newborn...

one *lover* to another

Chemical reactions in the brain can have you feeling like you are falling in love - when in fact you are just falling in lust - with the wrong guy.

Those initial moments, weeks and even months might have you deciding that he is 'The One' - the brain can play chemically induced tricks on your decision making process and can literally cause you to override the sensible, logical and practical side of your brain.

Now, this is not to say that the CHEMISTRY cannot be used to your advantage - those chemical reactions happen to both of you, so it is important to understand that a great connection can be formed and may flourish in those early days.

It is also important that you recognize and analyze the other, 'real' parts of this person whilst enjoying the thrill of that chemical high...

communication

COMMUNICATION is the *essence* to a great **connection**

Without COMMUNICATION, we do not have much of a relationship.

Without COMMUNICATION, we cannot possibly know what our partner wants, needs or feels.

Without COMMUNICATION, we are left feeling confused, ignored and irritated.

COMMUNICATION should flow easily; you should be able to express yourself without fear of ridicule or retribution, and you should be able to talk freely about matters that are important to you.

There is no point being with someone who does not make you feel heard and understood - if you cannot **communicate** your thoughts and feelings then your ability to **connect** is lost. But:

COMMUNICATION is a 2 way street -
                    you must be able to *express*
                                    AND to *listen*

Once you find that person with whom you can enjoy a conversation, delve into a discussion, express an emotion, then you have found a person with whom you can enjoy a lifelong **connection** filled with COMMUNICATION.

compatibility

For a relationship to have long term potential, you need to be compatible in the areas of your life that are important to you.

For example:

If **religion** or **spirituality** is important to you, most likely you'll want to attract a partner with similar beliefs.

If you are planning to have **children** or help raise step-children, are your views about child-rearing on the same wavelength?

What about how you view **money**? Is one person a spender and one a saver?

What about your **hobbies** - do you have an interest in common that you can do together? Anything from hiking to sailing to golfing to stamp collecting; it does not matter what it is but it matters that you have at least one similar interest.

Are you each close to your **family** members or does one have strained relationships and the other loves to spend every holiday with the family?

These are all COMPATIBILITY issues that need to be discussed if you sense a relationship might be moving toward a serious place - and even if you do not want to discuss them head on, it is advisable to ask questions about each issue and listen to his answers - they will tell you what you need to know and will save you heartache further down the line.

character

CHARACTER encapsulates morals and values.

CHARACTER could even be described as integrity.

Is the man you are with a man of good CHARACTER?

It is not only - "Is he a GOOD *match*?"

It should also be - "Is he a GOOD *person*?"

If you can trust him with small things, then you can probably trust him with bigger things too.

If he is there when you need a helping hand, then he is displaying good CHARACTER.
If he talks clearly and honestly about matters of importance, then you can judge his CHARACTER by his words and actions.

CHARACTER is displayed over time, it is demonstrated through actions, it is solidified with words that compliment those actions.

CHARACTER is one of the fundamental building blocks of a good man, and a great relationship.

Look for CHARACTER when looking for a man.

...the **hand** in **glove** of CONTINUITY

A relationship is like a hand, it has fingers that are able to function alone but work best when used in harmony - the strength of each finger is multiplied when used as a coherent team.

CONTINUITY is the glove that keeps that hand warm during the cold spells, the glove that protects that hand when picking up something with thorns, the glove that does not allow a chill to enter the bones of that hand when the rains fall or the snows arrive.

CONTINUITY IS THE *GLOVE*

THE 5 FINGERS ARE:

Social Activities & Hobbies
Emotional Connection
Economic Agreement
Family & Friends
Intimacy

Hobbies & Social Activities

There should be an easy connection
between the person you love
and the things you love to do.

This does not mean that you have to do everything together, or that you both have to love the exact same things, but it does mean that there should be an overlap - a place where you meet on common ground, where you spend time together, where you enjoy the activity with each other, where you **connect outside of**

yourselves, where you can **share meaningful experiences** and **create memories**.

It might be something as simple and mundane as loving the same television show; it could be something as crazy and wild as base jumping - whatever it might be, it must be there, and it must be genuine...

There is no point forcing your passion on your partner if they are miserable - there is no point taking him on a horse ride every weekend if he does not enjoy it, and there is no point pretending to love cars when they bore you to tears - that is just a good recipe for dissatisfaction and arguments.

The great thing about having overlapping hobbies is that you will most likely have a positive cross-over in the social aspects of your relationship as well - and that can only be a good thing for your love, because socializing creates a sense of belonging and a burden of proof for the COMMITMENT.

Emotional Connection

An EMOTIONAL CONNECTION is an ever-evolving, ever-pleasurable part of the COMMITMENT.

As the time rolls by and the experiences mount up, the EMOTIONAL CONNECTION between two compatible people will inevitably grow stronger and this

EMOTIONAL CONNECTION acts as an **added bond** in the relationship.

An EMOTIONAL CONNECTION may be determined by a number of factors - respect, mutual understanding, admiration, support, laughter, perceived intelligence...

This EMOTIONAL CONNECTION is not something that just exists, it needs to be nurtured and valued and it needs to be important for *each* partner, not only the work of one person - although one person can trigger the connection at any one time. In order to maintain an EMOTIONAL CONNECTION each partner must maintain **respect**, **integrity**, **honesty**, **clarity** and **love** with and for their partner so that each partner understands that they are important to the person they have placed EMOTIONAL importance upon.

The importance of an EMOTIONAL CONNECTION can never be underestimated in that it incorporates so many aspects of the mind that not only trigger love but also maintain that love, and if that EMOTIONAL CONNECTION is strong and healthy it will encourage each partner to be strong and healthy within the relationship also - once two people have settled into this EMOTIONAL CONNECTION they will find themselves more at peace in every part of their lives.

Economic Agreement

It does not matter who earns the most, or who spends what, so long as there is an agreement in terms of **spending, saving** and **showing**.
If one person loves to be extravagant and the other person is comfortable with that, then good for you.

If one person is frugal and the other a spend thrift, then you had better come to some kind of agreement pretty soon - either the spend thrift only spends their own money, or the frugal one offers up an allowance that must be fair and well-monitored.

There is nothing so dangerous to a relationship than **financial arguments** - and these arguments occur even when there is plenty of money to go round, let alone when money is tight and the family is divided.

The best case scenario is that you both have similar spending and saving habits - the worst case scenario is that the home-maker spends all the bread-winners money with little or no regard for the objects they purchase or the consequences of their actions.

The most important element of ECONOMIC AGREEMENT is that one party does not jeopardize the life and security of the other through their spending habits. Everything else is a matter of personal acceptance and **mutual** agreement.

Family & Friends

FAMILY & FRIENDS have your best interests at heart (I hope) - they want you to make wise choices, and they want you to be happy.
If your FRIENDS like your partner then you have hit a **home run** - if your FAMILY like him too then you have hit the **jackpot**.

If your partner gets along with your FAMILY & FRIENDS, then you are in **heaven**...

We have all heard the stories about the mother-in-law who creates havoc or the father-in-law who is disrespectful and rude; unfortunately these situations arise and if they do they need to be handled **openly** and **clearly** with an understanding from each of you that family is family and love is important.

Knowing what to expect always helps, and agreeing on how much time will be spent with FRIENDS, or which holidays will be spent with FAMILY can certainly assist in managing problems if they should exist.

In an ideal world we have a perfect balance of FAMILY & FRIENDS and time TOGETHER as a couple - so let's make a perfect world!

Intimacy

Without INTIMACY we lose the connection that creates happiness - and COMMITMENT means very little without happiness.

It is imperative to the longevity of your love that you **demonstrate** and **receive** INTIMACY.
The small things are just as important as the grand gestures - a **kiss** on the neck, **holding hands** at the table, **touching** each others knee whilst watching a movie, **looking** into each other's eyes, a **stroke** here, a **wink** there...

The basics of lovemaking and a powerful physical connection are also important, and these should be enjoyed **regularly** in order to maintain the physical connection and the emotional enjoyment.

There may be times when work stress or child-rearing come in between you and your partner - this is natural, but not insurmountable - during these times, the smaller gestures are sometimes the best forms of INTIMACY to enact because they require the least effort, they are the least intrusive, and they create a sense of **security** and **love**.

Physical and emotional INTIMACY are paramount for a successful relationship - each of these require constant nurturing and attention.

continuity...
LEADING TO commitment

CONTINUITY is about **consistency**, about working to create a flow in the relationship, about knowing that this other person is a part of your daily and weekly life, that the relationship has roots.

If there is CONTINUITY in a relationship, then there is a likelihood that each of you are working at building a strong relationship.

A strong relationship requires putting down roots so that you can survive the hurricanes that may pass your way from time to time.

CONTINUITY is an inherent factor in a great relationship

Family, friends, religious ideals, child-rearing ideas,

vacation options, financial circumstances, living experiences are all important factors to consider in maintaining a sense of CONTINUITY, because each of these are going to be relevant in the present and in the future.

You must both be comfortable about each others circumstances, and comfortable with each others beliefs if you are to continually enjoy and grow this relationship.

With continuity,
      you will naturally
            merge into *COMMITMENT.*

MEN, SEX & COMMITMENT

Does SEX = COMMITMENT?

Does COMMITMENT = SEX?

The short answer: NO

But that's okay... as long as you *know*.

I am a big believer in having your own ideas, boundaries, comfort zones and ideas about SEX.

SEX is such an intensely personal situation that there is no point in me trying to tell you what you should do, or what you should not do.

Having said this, I will offer up some thoughts for you to think about, some notions for you to notice, some ideas that might intrigue you...

MEN are VISUAL beings -
men want to turn their VISUAL *attraction*
into PHYSICAL *action*

For men - SEX & COMMITMENT are two separate entities -

A man can have SEX with a woman and he might not

see it as anything more than SEX.

- if a woman is willing to offer it... a man will usually take it -

But the points below should be noted...

- MEN *love* the chase.
- MEN *want* what they cannot have.
- MEN will *work* for what they do not think they deserve.

A man might be committed to having SEX, but SEX is not a relationship COMMITMENT.

- How does a woman best deal with SEX & COMMITMENT?

Assuming that you are interested in a man, my generalized view is that a woman does best when she is affectionate without being overly flirtatious, when she is sensual without being *immediately* sexual.

By this I mean -

-If he tries to take your hand - do not pull away.

-Look into his eyes when he talks.

-Compliment him when you can.

-Be light-hearted.

-Be grateful.

-Be female.

* These might seem like obvious 'instructions' but you would be amazed at how rarely they are utilized.

If a man feels that a woman values his presence, enjoys his conversation, is attracted to his style and is happy when she is with him, then that man will be more than willing to take his time before the SEX issue even arises.

"You can't know sexual compatibility unless you give it a test drive. You can gauge, assess, forecast, etc... but those can lead to a wrong conclusion."

k.p - facebook

If you are not interested in a man on a SEXual level, then move away.

If you are not sure whether SEX is part of the equation, then be cautious - but do not act frigid or come across as cold.

If you are excited to have SEX with him, then make it clear that you are attracted to him - but do not jump on him... yet!

Men will wait if they feel that there is a light at the end of the tunnel... Men will value the woman who values herself... and values him.

Men want SEX to be special too - and if they don't, then they are the wrong man for you...Although there are a number of variables in any relationship, these variables are far more significant when it comes to SEX.

There needs to be a fine balance,

a delicate maneuvering
            between showing interest
                        and accepting his advances

Men are often caught between desire and manners when it comes to SEX - they might want to wait, but feel that this could place them in the 'friend zone', or they might want to advance with you sexually yet understand that it is too soon...

All in all,
        *men enjoy **some** guidance from women*

If a woman makes it clear, by subtle verbaliz
physical actions, then a man will know that
'wasting his time' and he will make sure to keep
in check.

If a man makes a move too soon, then a woman can
gently refuse the advance without losing the
momentum of his interest - she just has to say
something like, "Not yet... but soon" - this clarifies **her**
interest without killing **his** desire. A woman should be
in control of when and where SEX will occur, but she
should let the man take control during the act.

Although a man may want a COMMITMENT, SEX does
not guarantee that COMMITMENT - unless he is friends
with friends or even friends with family, there is no
reason for a man to feel that the sexual act has
anything to do with longevity or relationship or
COMMITMENT... to him, it is simply SEX... for now.

*"Expectation is the mother of disaster
Desperation is the sister."*

guy blews

73

THE STAGES OF COMMITMENT

In any situation that involves a relationship there are certain levels of commitment that occur before moving in, or marriage. These are some of the stages you might pass (in no particular order)

- Exclusive dating

- Exclusive sex (monogamy)

- Planning future trips together

- Planning a joint party at one of your homes

- Surviving emotional storms in a relationship

- Official Facebook relationship status (yes, really)

- Keys to their place and giving them keys to yours

- Accompanying each other to work events / parties

- Regular time together and regular sex with one another

- Introduction to family and friends or even boss & co-workers

- Space in their closet or drawer for clothes, toothbrushes etc...

- Activities with family and friends (it's one thing to introduce, it's another to do regular activities)

- Buying items together, including furniture, homes etc... and playing house by being involved in each others home life

- Maybe even working together or starting a business together

With each of these stages, each partner offers or accepts more and more responsibility with the other partner -

By discussing and agreeing to **monogamy**, both partners agree to make the effort and grow their connection.

By **introducing** a partner to people who are important, one steps up to the connection and the other accepts.

By using or offering a drawer or a closet one offers up **space** and the offer is accepted.

By accepting the **keys**, one (or both) offers up trust and the trust is accepted.

By **investing** in possessions each partner offers up their financial (and in some ways emotional) commitment to the other.

All of the above are signs and agreements that this relationship is special, that each partner sees it as having potential and that each partner is willing to make the commitment necessary to find **longevity** and **consistency** in the love that they have both found.

Men, in particular, do not always want to step up to the commitment initially, but if a woman can introduce each stage as being beneficial to **him**_, to_ **his life**_, to_ **their love** _then he will be more willing to go that extra mile in order that he does not have to live without the woman he loves._

COMMITMENT
versus PROMISE

action VERSUS words

A man means what he says... when he says it.

But if a man does not follow through on his spoken words, he has not made the commitment.

If the action does not occur, then the promise was not met.

---

a **promise** *is not a* **commitment**

a **promise** - verbally stated future intention to perform a specific act:

I promise to pick up your dry cleaning.

I promise to be exclusive in our relationship.

a commitment :

-a fact demonstrated by behavior

-an ATTITUDE consisting of thoughts and beliefs

I am committed to keeping my promises

I am committed to our relationship

a **promise** is something you *say*
a **commitment** is something you *do*

---

*a **promise** is situation specific*
*a **commitment** is contextual*

A promise is a small, verbal commitment...

However - if a potential partner does NOT keep PROMISES, it is wise to question their ability to keep COMMITMENTS...

PROMISES & COMMITMENTS ARE RELATED *just as* WORDS & ACTIONS ARE RELATED

YOU ARE **NOT** IN A COMMITTED RELATIONSHIP IF:

1. You are **not sure** if this relationship is committed.

You and your partner have not **formalized** your relationship as committed.

You and your partner are **not in agreement** about the

status of your relationship.

Your friends and family view the status of your relationship **differently** than you do.

You are **projecting** your wishes onto the situation without them being realized.

The **words** of commitment are not being supported by the **actions** of commitment.

- _a commitment is explicit and unambiguous_

-_a commitment is a formal event of some kind between two people_

- _a commitment is something you DO over time_

- _a real commitment has consequences for breaking it_

For a relationship to be truly committed, there are no exits - _mentally, emotionally,_ or _physically._

Relationships are never clear cut and easy - there is always a **dance** that comes with love, fun, sex, longevity, continuity and commitment - this **dance** requires each partner to be _present, aware_ and _alive_ within the relationship.

Without the **dance** - a continual movement and transference of energy - we are only left with a stagnant situation that is not conducive to true, exciting, heart-warming, powerful love.

The **dance of love** is the best way to keep your man interested and interesting, to show that you are capable but also vulnerable enough to ignite his desire, to enjoy the intimate moments whilst always knowing that the reality of daily life is something that cannot be avoided.

The **dance of love** is, above all, about balance - about balancing out excitement with seriousness, fun with finances, newness with comfort, longevity with loving.

"It doesn't matter if the guy is perfect or the girl is perfect, as long as they are perfect for each other."

good will hunting

* See references

THE 6
MAIN KINDS OF MEN

nice guys & bad boys   THE romancer

MAN WITH issues   mental MAN

THE AWAKENING MAN

nice guys & bad boys

As much as women might say they are looking for a "good man", and as understandable as that may seem, what exactly is a good man?

Is it a bad boy? The manly type who seems to challenge society's norms, who takes risks, who lives life on the edge.

Is it a **nice guy**? The more delicate version of the species who may be *good*, but not manly.

bad boys are usually the ones who set off the chemical attraction - they are brimming with confidence - they set the trend - they state their case - they are not swayed by others - they need nobody - they choose their path.

nice guys are most often too 'nice' for their own good - they come across as friend material - they follow the herd - they do not think originally - there are no surprises - their social graces may be a little too timid - they do not stand out from the crowd.

bad boys are dangerous

                                    nice guys are the family type
bad boys buck the system

                                    nice guys fit into the norm
bad boys break the rules

                                    nice guys follow the rules

If a bad boy is not particularly good looking, he can be sexy...

If a **nice guy** is handsome, he might come across as 'square'...

The bad boy has the edge in the beginning, he is more likely to stray later on and disregard his responsibilities.

The **nice guy** will probably provide sustenance, shelter and an education for his children and his wife.

The bad boy has trained himself to not care - but sometimes this boy can be great for a casual, transitional and fun relationship for the woman not ready for a serious relationship.

The **nice guy** has been trained to be respectful, kind and caring - his life mechanism is one of thinking before acting, taking on the responsibilities presented and following through on the decisions he makes.

Nothing in life is black and white, but when it comes to

bad boys and **nice guys,** the good part of the bad boy will probably fade away and the good part of the nice guy is inclined to make him stay.

THE romancer

Just because he is romantic does not mean he is good for you.

Many a romancer has tricked his way into a woman's boudoir only to leave in the middle of the night without a backward glance. THE romancer is too good to be true - he texts, emails and calls when he says he will; he speaks the language that you understand, he appeases your emotions, he feeds you with interest and excitement and he makes you feel special.

THE romancer
     will woo, wow and whisk you away
          for a moment or two

The dangerous part about this man is that he actually **loves the idea of being in love** and he really believes that he is looking for THE ONE. The reality of THE romancer is that he does not have the ability to sustain a relationship. He gets off on the thrill of the first date excitement, the first night together, the chemical high and the illusion - but once reality bites, once the chemical high of dopamine has worn off, once there is a storm to deal with, he is looking for yet another love of his life.

And that's how you spot THE romancer - he has a string of previous relationships that he does not seem at all cut up about because he was never really that invested in the first place.

THE romancer appears to be actively seeking a relationship when in actual fact he is simply responding to an intense attraction to someone new - he verbalizes this attraction and follows those words with romantic actions... for a while.

He may seem sensitive, and he may well be extremely seductive - in fact, he will do whatever is necessary to cement an involvement, but once the chase is over, THE romancer is gone.

Ultimately, THE romancer is just laying the groundwork for passionate, complicated and short-lived dalliances that leave all parties frustrated.

However, if THE romancer somehow manages to weather a storm and overcome a relationship problem, he might just land on top of you and stay there because he has found HIS ONE - this might happen because of his age, it might happen because of an event that shook him up, or it might just be you.

There is no knowing what will make THE romancer fall for you; but if he does, then you are one lucky girl!

MAN WITH issues

As much as I wish we did not have to confront this, it would be remiss of me to ignore it.

Ladies, there are a multitude of men out there who have issues.

BIG issues

Of course, nobody is perfect, but a MAN WITH issues is not to be messed with - he will only take you down with him, in the most insensitive way possible.

MAN WITH issues might have clinical issues - he could be bi-polar, depressive, angry.

MAN WITH issues might have had a crash in his life, a mid-life crisis that still haunts him.

MAN WITH issues might dabble in or rely upon alcohol and drugs.

MAN WITH issues might have a gambling addiction, or even a sex addiction.

MAN WITH issues can start off as being great fun, he might laugh alot, he might be adventurous, he may even be the life of the party - but when the alcohol or drugs wear off it is a whole different story.

Getting involved with MAN WITH issues is a gamble... But many women try to fix this man, they think they can be his savior, they want to feel worthy in his eyes - as with all gambles, the odds are NOT tipped in your favor.

MAN WITH issues might appear to be working on himself by constantly talking about what he has achieved and what he needs to do... when in fact, he is still lost and weak.

The tell- tale signs of MAN WITH issues come from his erratic and inconsistent behavior, his aggressive and extreme mood swings, his inability to actually carry out what he states, and his avoidance of really being an active and involved partner in your relationship. There really is very little upside to MAN WITH issues because he is riddled with problems that he is either refusing to confront or he is unable to move through. MAN WITH issues is stuck.

If MAN WITH issues is funny you will only end up laughing at him - not with him.

If MAN WITH issues is depressed you will only end up looking after him - he will never look after you.

My advice: Avoid MAN WITH issues - you deserve better than that.
Avoid MAN WITH issues by being honest with yourself about who he *really* is.

mental MAN

The mental MAN is logical, linear and learned. Some people might describe him as a geek- He is definitely the intellectual type

He likes to read books, he is a 'brainiac', an academic - he might well be a computer whizz - he knows what he is good at and he sticks to it, either by reaching the P.H.D level of recognition or by picking up on a new technology or invention and becoming an expert or entrepreneur in that field.

mental MAN is not good at sports and so he steers clear of most strenuous or skilled competitive activity that involves hand-eye co-ordination or physical exertion - this does not mean that he is unfit as he might be a hiker, a cyclist or even a runner.

His mind is his strongest asset and so he does not process emotions through his heart - in fact, he shuts down in the face of emotions - yet he seems to be in calm control of himself and therefore offers a comparative safety to his partner - although it should be noted that mental MAN will most likely seek a love built on companionship.

For the right type of woman - a woman that mental MAN can respect intellectually - this man offers a relaxed, drama free existence filled with interesting conversation and a sense of stability that tends to create an aura of comfort and quiet security.

mental MAN is often aloof, wrapped up in the latest invention, idea or conundrum that might have crossed his path.

He is the man who does not connect well with others - this does not mean he is not a good, genuine, kind individual, it simply means that he does not react emotionally or connect emotionally in the way that a woman might wish for - and he never will.

If a woman can accept that this relationship will not be overly demonstrative or affectionate, and if she does not mind being a support system for a man who may well have intense connections to inanimate pursuits, then mental MAN could be a good fit.

A relationship with mental MAN has every chance of longevity because it is built in a calm, quiet and solid way - she knows where she stands and she understand him... he knows that she is there so he will be a stable and dependable mate.

THE AWAKENING MAN

This is, of course, the man who we would all like to meet, and the man we would all like to be (if we are men).

THE AWAKENING MAN is usually older - although there are examples (few and far between) of younger men AWAKENING despite their relative inexperience... I think some people call them 'old souls'.

THE AWAKENING MAN has been through the ringer, has experienced the ups and downs of life, has worked on what went wrong, has learned the lessons and is now choosing the path of self-discovery and enlightenment.

THE AWAKENING MAN is in touch with himself and is therefore able to give freely and lovingly to the woman in his life, a woman he chooses to be with because she **enhances** his existence, she **brightens** his day, she adds **positively** to his life.

This is the man that women dream of - his confidence is appealing, his intelligence attractive, his demeanor almost intoxicating - he is *sexy*.

He has reached a point in his life where he can accept criticism as constructive and he can make his point without being destructive.

THE AWAKENING MAN has space in his life and he enjoys that space without fear.

THE AWAKENING MAN has goals in his life and he pursues those goals without desperation.

THE AWAKENING MAN can listen to what you say, but above all he hears what you say and acts upon those words - he will hold your hand when you need him to, he will be resolute and steadfast when the storms of life and of love come your way.

There is **no** power struggle with THE AWAKENING MAN, there is **no** competition - when he says "I love you", he truly means it, because his love includes this caveat -

I AM HERE. YOU MATTER. WE ARE IMPORTANT

THE AWAKENING MAN wants to grow with the woman he loves and he wants to raise his game in order that the love between you will grow.

If you are to enjoy THE AWAKENING MAN you should be an AWAKENING WOMAN - for the THE AWAKENING MAN is not the man that wants to fix you, he is the man that wants to enjoy you; he is at a point in his life where he does not have time to play games or argue over the little things, even though he will support you in your endeavors and he will respect you for your sense of self-achievement.

All in all, THE AWAKENING MAN is the cream of the crop, he is the top of the tree, he is the man you should be looking for, the man to set you free."

- that rhymes!

THE WAY MEN TALK

Men are not always the best talkers... or listeners.

In fact, they can be downright terrible when it comes to expressing themselves and allowing you to express yourself.

The problem is that men do not like **confrontation...**
and they do not enjoy **explanation**

Whereas a woman will want to work through her feelings by verbalizing so that she can come to an understanding, a man will not.

Allow me to demonstrate through analogy :
When a woman goes shopping she will generally walk through the store picking out what she likes and holding it up; she might then try it on and if she likes it she will imagine all the situations that she could / would / might wear these items - then she will jump in and purchase (even if it needs to be tailored a little).

a woman likes to browse and then make a decision

When a man goes shopping, he walks in the store, tells the assistant what size he is, waits for her to get it and then he buys it and walks out - no thought or emotion is involved because it is a transaction of an item that will keep him warm...

a man wants to deal with the purchase and move on

I know I am generalizing, but in general, women are **emotional** and men are **not** - therefore, women will take much more time to process a situation and men will move away from it - especially if it is uncomfortable.

By understanding that men are not good at 'wallowing' in the moment (whether it be extreme pleasure or extreme pain), a woman can understand why men are not good at sharing their feelings.

Many men have been raised to not express their feelings - it is regarded as a weakness which means that women have to deal with a partner who might not be very demonstrative. If a man does demonstrate his love, it is usually a big deal - and a woman should recognize this, thank him and **encourage** more behavior of a similar nature by gently cajoling him to feel comfortable about what he did...

Added to this, women would do well to react mildly to a man's 'revelations' (whether good or bad) so that he is not 'spooked' by the reaction (whether overly joyous or overtly sedate).

Men want their woman to be happy, and they want their life to be easy, which means they would rather move on from the hysteria than wallow in the emotion of it all.

This might be a tough lesson to learn, an unpleasant truth to face... but, again, it is just the way men are.

THE TRUTH ABOUT DATING

I want you to meet the right man for you.

I want to help you in your search for love, and in so doing, I have to ask you **5** questions that will highlight whether you are *helping* or *hurting* yourself in this quest.

Are you sending out the right energy to meet *a* right man? For you to meet someone, your *mindset* must be in a place where you are able to cope with *including* someone in your life, a place that allows you to **accept** someone else into your world, a place that welcomes him.

Is your lifestyle conducive to dating right now? If you are overwhelmed by *responsibilities*, health issues, children, family or financial woes you might not have the stamina or the time to make the effort to meet someone. If this is the case, then perhaps you should be looking for the CASUAL relationship which offers _companionship_ and _intimacy_ without the need for a full on **commitment**.

What are your deal-breakers? Are you always trying to meet a 10 and in the process you overlook all the other great guys out there that would do you a world of good? It is important to keep your deal-breakers in line with your reality, to accept that nobody is perfect and to look for what is best for you _right now_ - you never know where a new man may take you - emotionally and physically.

Are you making opportunities to meet men? It is always a good idea to put yourself in the _line of fire_ when it comes to men - go to networking groups, singles mixers, gourmet dining groups; involve yourself in hobbies like skiing and golf that naturally allow you to meet men. Spending time at _home_, working from _home_, raising kids in the _home_ is detrimental to getting yourself seen and found - volunteer work, your place of worship, even business meetings in other areas give you the chance to make **connections** and will open up the playing field of opportunity.

Are you flexible? Being too _rigid_ with what type of man you have to have, or how he has to behave might be hindering your chances of connecting with someone great. Look back at your past relationships - if you are repeating the same mistakes it might be an idea to change up the pace, try another race. This does not mean lower your standards, it means **change** the course, open your mind, be more flexible.

Settling for a less-than-man is not the right thing to do for you... or for him. If you cannot seem to get away from a COMPANIONSHIP or a COMPLACENCY relationship, then you might need to ask yourself why -

What energy are you putting out there that attracts these men?
What is it about you that is stopping you from finding what you really want in a man?

Reflect on your patterns of behavior and see what changes you can make in your emotions, your energy, your lifestyle to set yourself up more successfully to be a match to the right man and the best relationship.

THE TRUTH is that a successful relationship is found and enjoyed when we step back and observe ourselves as much as we stand up and view others. It requires honesty and soul-searching, but in the end THE TRUTH will set you free and THE TRUTH will be your friend.

"Take time to be sure, but be sure not to take too much time"   anon

7 TYPES OF RELATIONSHIPS

FOR THE SAKE OF EASE AND FOR YOU TO HAVE A GOOD IDEA OF WHAT TO EXPECT AND WHAT YOU MIGHT HAVE TO DEAL WITH, I HAVE DIVIDED RELATIONSHIPS WITH MEN INTO 7 CATEGORIES.

SOME OF THESE MIGHT BE PERFECT FOR YOU RIGHT NOW (BUT NOT IN THE FUTURE), SOME OF THESE MIGHT BE PERFECT FOR YOU IN THE FUTURE (BUT NOT RIGHT NOW), SOME OF THESE MIGHT MAKE NO SENSE TO YOU AT ALL, SOME OF THESE MIGHT OVERLAP, SOME OF THESE MIGHT BE A PART OF YOUR HISTORY - IF THEY ARE I HOPE YOU HAVE LEARNED THE LESSON (IF YOU HAVEN'T THEN HERE'S A SECOND CHANCE).

EACH RELATIONSHIP HAS IT'S POSITIVES AND NEGATIVES, JUST AS EACH MAN HAS HIS POSITIVES AND NEGATIVES, JUST AS EACH WOMAN HAS HERS.

READ THESE WITH AN OPEN MIND AND TAKE FROM THEM WHATEVER IT IS THAT HELPS YOU...

7 TYPES OF RELATIONSHIPS:
family life
dependent
she's in control
he's in control
companionship
casual
conscious

-family life

This is the relationship with the man who wants to be part of a family - he is the guy who is heavily involved in coaching the kids soccer league even if he is not a dad...

He is also the guy who loves to throw a ball around with his children or nephews and nieces on the weekend.

family life is the relationship you will experience with the guy who enjoys the energy and the inclusion of family - he thrives on the whole experience of a close knit family unit, the feeling of being part of something bigger than himself.

If you are the type of woman that wants to be a step mom, or are looking for a great guy to help with your own children, the family life guy might just be the one for you. Activities are his strong suit, creating family style memories are his specialty, being active and energized are part of his existence.

His ability to juggle his work life with his family life is impressive - he seems to have hours in the day that nobody else can find and he knows the importance of being there for the younger generation.

The guy who loves the family life might not be the most romantic, or even the most sensitive guy on the block - in fact, he may put the overall family way ahead of intimacy and romance, but all in all, the guy who loves family life is a good guy, a supportive guy, a handy guy to have around.

- dependent

The dependent male goes from one long term relationship to another - he might even jump into marriage for no apparent reason after one long term relationship ended... to the dismay of his Ex-Girlfriend.

A man who thrives in a dependent relationship is not necessarily a bad guy, he just needs to be with someone - for example, he might find it hard to be alone, be overtly communicative, suffer from low self-esteem, be defined by his relationship.

The dependent male is easily activated by fear of abandonment and may well be *more attached to the relationship and not the individual they are partnered with*, which means they will work hard at keeping the relationship going - however this can sometimes reveal itself as **jealousy, anger** and **possessiveness**.

These characteristics may often make a woman feel extremely important, but he might also display a higher level of intrusion by looking through texts, phone or emails to allay his fears and insecurities.

Although the dependent male bases his love and affection on fear, he can also be extremely loving and available, which might work well with a woman who is looking to be in an insular, communicative and extremely physically and emotionally monogamous relationship.

- she's in control

This is the relationship where the woman is the alpha

and the man is the beta - he is the wind beneath her wings, her biggest fan.

She is strong, she is in command and he totally respects her - he supports her dreams and contributes to making them become a reality.

The she's in control relationship works best with a weaker male - the less dominant or submissive male who is attracted to this woman can make for an excellent match.

How come?

Gratitude - he feels lucky to be with a powerful woman, he admires her, even worships her, he places her on a pedestal and he will be loyal.

Do not overlook a man who, at first glance, may not be the best looking or smoothest guy in the room if you are the type of woman who knows what she wants and knows how to get it - oftentimes, the men that are attracted to a she's in control female are the men that treat women exceptionally well because they value their partner and are well aware that she has the choice to be with someone else.

If she's in control tries to pair up with an alpha male, the combination can be explosive, unpleasant and doomed to fail - an alpha female may well do best with a beta male.

With the she's in control female, the beta male must be sure to satisfy her in the bedroom, or he will lose her to a man that can - this is where the beta male must excel.

- he's in control

If he's in control, he thinks of *his* woman as a piece of property, a trophy, an ego boost.

he's in control wants a woman who is soft, feminine and undemanding, whom he has power over - she must be submissive and allow him to get his way. This man does not want to change, he does not want to be fixed. These men are often highly successful, high testosterone guys whose jealousy can spiral into physical violence, whose interest can turn into intrusion of your every waking moment.

He will have high expectations and his rules will be rigidly enforced, he is easily disappointed - but he will be your protector, he will take care of things, he will take care of you... for a price.

When he's in control it can be extremely intoxicating because the romance is full on, the sex is powerful, the make ups and break ups addictive, the gifts overwhelming, the apologies endearing and the irrationality confusing. As much as there are elements of passion, power and possessions with this man, the price you pay for the upside is unlikely to be worth the price you pay on the down swing.

Women who get involved when he's in control are often drawn to him because he represents a father figure, a figure of dominance, a figure of security - and he knows this so he uses it to his advantage by pushing his control to the limits.

This is a dangerous relationship to become embroiled in, and not one I would recommend for the long term.

- companionship

A relationship based on companionship is a relationship built on a solid foundation of mutual interest, understanding and friendship.

This relationship might even have evolved from a

friendship, which is always a good starting point.

This couple enjoys their time together, they play well together, they work well together, they make a good team in the parental field as well.

The companionship male is calm. He can be romantic, but he will not be original. He may even be intimate and affectionate on occasion, but most of all he will simply be kindly, honest and true.
This is not a relationship built on lust or libido, and if the sexual chemistry is weak, then the sex life might be infrequent, but this is not necessarily detrimental to longevity because the most important component of this situation is the friendship.

If you are looking for something comfortable and easy, this might be the type of relationship that works for you - there will be no jealousy, no arguments, no drama - in fact, there will be little to worry about because the premise is one of loyalty and companionship.

Life will be easy... if slightly sedated.

- casual

This is a popular, modern type of relationship - society no longer views the casual relationship as unsavory - in fact, I would argue that most relationships start off this way.

Perhaps both participants are working, maybe they have children or are caring for elderly parents

In many cases, the casual relationship is quite practical:

With an abundance of intimacy, fun, companionship, romance, communication, excitement, variation and time apart, there is less likelihood of jealousy or complacency setting in.
Having someone to go to a concert with, have dinner and drinks with, have sex with, travel with, is all upside... as long as you are realistic, have no expectations, and take it slow - there is no long term commitment on the radar in the beginning.

- The **biggest** desire is FREEDOM
- The **biggest** fear is CONSTRAINT

For a man, this is a light-hearted and enjoyable

situation that might morph into something more over time... as long as there is no pressure from you.

For a woman, this relationship might lead to emotional attachment - it is important that she is honest with herself about what this relationship truly is, and that she enjoys it for that - if it grows into something more, lucky her. The casual relationship is a nice interval after a divorce, a tester to re-learn what might have been forgotten in a marriage, a fun experience that might lead nowhere, or might go somewhere great...

- conscious

We come to the ideal relationship - the relationship built with the conscious male - the man who has processed his life, taken control of his issues, and has cleared the path for building a great, loving, long term relationship.

This is the relationship with the man who wants to be with you, who loves and adores you, who knows when to be the man and allows you to be YOU.

If you have a disagreement in this relationship it is dealt with in a communicative and constructive way, you work through your problems as a team - and your love grows stronger through the understanding because you hold hands through the storms and you even work through your own issues together.

The conscious relationship is built on mutual **respect**, and thrives on mutual **appreciation, attention** and **affection**.

A conscious relationship fully incorporates the **5 C's** -

chemistry, communication, character, compatibility & continuity

The conscious relationship involves a blending of each other's lives, freely and easily.

The only issue is this - if you are not ready to be with this man, then you should wait. If you are dealing with a divorce, working two jobs, raising small children, looking after your parents or have other life courses that need to be overcome, then this conscious male may not be the man for you... yet. But once you have moved into your right zone, a conscious relationship awaits.

RELATIONSHIPS &
the MEN who choose them

- family life
nice guys / mental MAN / THE AWAKENING MAN

- dependent
THE romancer / MAN WITH issues

- she's in control
nice guys / MAN WITH issues

- he's in control
bad boy / MAN WITH issues

- companionship
nice guys / mental MAN / THE AWAKENING MAN

- casual
bad boy / MAN WITH issues / THE romancer

- conscious
THE AWAKENING MAN

"If you live to be a hundred I want to live to be a hundred minus a day so I don't have to live a day without you."
winnie-the-pooh

KEYS TO THE KINGDOM

As a woman seeking a long term commitment from a man, you should have these **4 keys** on your keychain, and you should use them regularly to open the relevant doors of a man's desire. You see, if a man feels desire, then he will always stick around.

These are the 4 keys TO THE KINGDOM of MEN...

FEED

F*CK

FUEL

FUN

Yes, it is that **simple**...

It is that **basic**...

Open each of these **doors** and you will be blessed with a happy, fulfilling, long term love - you will maintain his interest, heighten his desire, excite his imagination and satisfy his wants, needs and yearnings.

FEED = key 1

FEED his love.

The way to a man's heart is through his stomach, *and* through his mind.

If you do not FEED a man, he will wither and die - and so will his love.

If you keep a man fed, if he knows where to get his daily bread, if he understands that you understand how important he is and you feed him with love, then he will always come to you for nourishment...

and in return he will nourish you.

If you have any doubt as to the seriousness of what I am saying, look at the man whose mother adores him...

Look at how he maintains a close connection with his mother because she knows how to FEED him on a regular basis.

Look at the way he returns to his mother like a little boy - this is the man who understands that to FEED him is *nurture* as much as it is *nature*.

Need I say more?

FEED your man's heart with love and he will love you in return.

F*CK = key 2

I have to strip this down to its basic level so that you do not fall into the trap of so many other relationships.

This F is the 2nd KEY TO THE KINGDOM

Sex is one thing- **Making Love** is another
Foreplay is extremely important...

BUT: This F is what needs to be continued throughout a relationship if you are to maintain the interest of your man.

*To men, the word F*CK is*

raw energy meeting sensuality
Too many relationships fade into a system of sex that

does not really stimulate either partner - for a man, the word F*CK shows a man how much the woman he loves **desires** him.

You would be amazed how arousing "I want to F*CK you" is to a man - as a whisper, a passing comment, a statement.

It is about keeping up the excitement, the fun, the 'je ne sais quoi' of your sex life so that he wants you *and only you*.

If the intimacy you share with your man becomes too mechanical or too sweet then you will likely lose him to another. I rest my case.

* please excuse my use of this word - it was necessary in order that I made the point loud and clear

FUEL = key 3

Men are ego based.

Men need to feel like a champion.

More specifically, men want to be *your* champion.

How best to make him feel this way?

FUEL his ego...

Compliment him.
Appreciate him.
Respect him.

If it requires you to think up ways that he can be a man so that you can then tell him how strong and wonderful and amazing you think he is - then do it.

If it means you have to ask him to carry the shopping or fix a light switch so you can tell him how impressed you are - then be sure to ask.

If it involves a little exaggeration in order that he gets the point - then exaggerate away.

Physical, mental, verbal... **whatever it takes to** *FUEL* **his ego - *do it*.**

FUN = key 4

Love is fruitless without light-heartedness.

Life is empty without laughter.

Friendships fade without FUN.

Know when to make a moment memorable with a laugh.

Know when to turn to him and smile.

Know when to look at him and wink.
Know when to touch him in public.

Know that softness is attractive and hardness is hard to endure.

Know that injecting playfulness into your life will make your love flower and bloom.

Know that FUN is an essential ingredient for a man to *want* you, to want to *be* with you, to want to *stay* with you.

No matter what responsibilities come your way,
FUN is free and FUN is your friend... & his.

Your Soul Mate comes into your life to teach you lessons. Your True Love goes to school with you every day holding hands~

jonathon aslay

THE POWER OF 3

I want you to remember **THE POWER OF 3** in your search for a committed relationship –

3 DATES

3 WEEKS

3 MONTHS

3 QUARTERS

- 3 DATES

After your initial meeting with a man, you should always look at 3 DATES as a barometer for your future possibilities - not 1 date, not even 2 (unless he is so awful you cannot take anymore!) but a full 3 DATES...

In the first 3 DATES, you will be able to see all a man's 'tells' if you ask questions and wait for his responses.
The first 3 DATES are the time when we all put on our best game face, but even with that game face on, the truth will be available - from the little things, such as opening doors, how he treats the waiter, whether he listens to your actual response; through to the bigger things such as his relationship with family, the way he talks about his friends, his views on life...

Now, just because he does not have *everything* you might want on your check list, the first 3 DATES are the time when you check to see if has the essentials - good manners, a pleasant demeanor, timely attitude, respect for others, a strong core belief system...

If, in the first 3 DATES you notice gaping holes in his moral code, then you have permission to walk, but only when you think it may impact your safety or your sanity - other issues, such as marriage and children should not be primary factors on these dates - these dates are character searches more than agenda certifiers.

3 DATES in 3 WEEKS, and you are off to a good start - space with consistency *without* desperation. If you have more than 3 dates and it feels right, then good for you... but make sure to keep a little space between you so he knows you have your own life and other important goals.

- 3 MONTHS

Assuming that the first 3 DATES are a success, you can now step into the next phase.

Many men will explode like a rocket when they are 'into' a woman, they will pull out all the stops and come across as adoring and keen - *be warned* - this might be a chemically induced high that can quickly disappear.

Hence, the importance of 3 MONTHS - the **90 day** probation...

If a man can come down from the initial high (or afterglow) and still be the man he sold you in the beginning, you are on the right path.

If he suddenly changes within these 3 MONTHS - becomes more distant, is less available, answers calls less frequently, appears to lose the spark, then you know that this is not relationship material... But that's okay, it was a lesson learned, an experience gained, wisdom stored.

Humans are naturally designed to rush into situations of the heart - and more often than not it is emotionally detrimental.

We are chemically imbalanced when we find someone desirable - our brains take over and the surge we feel makes us think _fantasy_ instead of _reality_... When the chemical high subsides, many of us are left rejected, dejected and confused because "It was going so well and then all of a sudden..."
The first 3 MONTHS will be that time when you both decide whether you are compatible for a long term love - once the rush of chemicals calms down, the realization of what this means will begin to set in.

3 QUARTERS [9 Months]

3 QUARTERS is the time when the truth will surface, when reality is accepted, when the chemicals no longer hide what is really there, when an argument or too many will occur - it might be over personality, the future, family, behavior, desire, or the dishes... Whatever these arguments are, the way they are handled will tell you what you need to know about this man...

Sometimes the man will evaporate, other times the woman will no longer see what she saw before.

Men find it easier to walk away - but they will stay if they feel that the woman they are with is worth the 'fight' because she understands him, loves him, fuels him...

Women are already invested - and sometimes this means they stay even when the red flags are flying high...

It is wise to be honest in these moments and see what is truly going on; do not let yourself hold on to *how he was* because you want to be with someone, realize *what he is*, what he truly is (is he right for you?)

If he is a gentleman, a good guy, a decent person, it is wise to invest in this man, to build your relationship in those 3 QUARTERS and let your guard down a little at a time as the love transitions from something new to something more certain.

"I love that you get cold when it is 71 degrees out.
I love that it takes you an hour and a half to order a sandwich.
I love that you get a little crinkle in your nose when you're looking at me

like I'm nuts.
I love that after I spend the day with
you, I can still smell your perfume on
my clothes. And I love that you are the
last person I want to talk to before I go
to sleep at night. And it's not because
I'm lonely, and it's not because it's New
Year's Eve. I came here tonight because
when you realize you want to spend the
rest of your life with somebody, you
want the rest of your life to start as
soon as possible"

when harry met sally

The ULTIMATE CONNECTION

Everything you have read in this book has been working towards helping you find a more altruistic, far superior, far more pleasurable relationship based upon creating a great CONNECTION that grows into something deep and meaningful - when you truly *connect* with this man and he completely *connects* with you.

This is THE ULTIMATE CONNECTION - where you are able to disagree like adults, work through your issues, respect each other's point of view, stimulate each other's mind and body, and connect on a level that is sustainable and enjoyable.

ULTIMATELY, no relationship, no marriage, no love is going to survive without going through some rough times, some awkward situations, some uncomfortable moments - it is in these times that we learn about ourselves and our partner; it is at these moments that our relationship can grow and evolve into something that develops strong roots which enable it to flourish in the future because there is a mutual respect, an understanding, a workability, a CONNECTION.

I have offered you 7 *jewels* that will help you find, build, grow and maintain this ULTIMATE CONNECTION -

-the 7 *jewels*

1 - MEN ARE *NOT* COMMITMENT PHOBIC

2 TYPES OF (AVAILABLE) MEN

THE POWER OF **3**

4 keys TO THE KINGDOM

The **5** C's

the **6** *main* kinds of MEN

7 TYPES OF RELATIONSHIPS

Each of these gives you an overview of what **is** and **is not** acceptable in love, what **should** and **should not** be expected of men, what **can** and **cannot** be achieved with those men, what **will** and **will not** work for the men you invite into your life. I hope they prove invaluable.

In CONCLUSION...

I have attempted to show you, in the clearest way possible, that MEN really *do* want to be in love, and that MEN really *do* want to be in relationships.

As much as the methods and needs of MEN and WOMEN may appear to be different, in reality we are all inspired by encouragement, we are all excited by touch, and we are all looking for appreciation and love.

I hope that UNDERSTAND MEN NOW has perhaps triggered some ideas for you to work with, has given you tools to utilize, and has offered hope to nurture your inspiration when it comes to MEN and relationships.

I wish you the very best in your search for a long lasting and fruitful love with the man you so richly deserve in order that the life you build together is filled to the brim with peace, warmth and happiness.

JONATHON ASLAY

ABOUT THE AUTHOR:

Jonathon Aslay

Dating is a challenge for everyone. Regardless of age or circumstance, we all struggle to find our perfect match. As someone who has graduated with honors from life's virtual University of Dating, Jonathon Aslay assists women in finding that seemingly elusive man with whom they can have both compatibility and passion.

Jonathon knows the male brain. He listens to women and what they want. Most importantly, he is gifted at bridging the gap between the two. As a "guy's guy", he committed years ago in the wake of his divorce to forever persevere along the path of self–knowledge and growth. Part of the process began as a tentative re–entry, followed by a full–blown immersion into, the dating world.

Through dating and discussion of dating experiences with fellow singles, Jonathon not only learned volumes about himself, but developed a network of close friendships with men and women likewise seeking to "choose better" when it came to life partners.

As Jonathon found men and women gravitating towards him with tales of their dating encounters, he started to see patterns in the things women complained about most, and those that continually baffled men. Over time, he realized that processing information from both sides and combining them with his own dating experiences enabled him to filter out the interpersonal "noise" that often causes people to invest in someone who is wrong for them. In short, he utilized the clarity and resulting confidence that had fueled his own personal growth to assist others in their relationships. Jonathon's career as a dating coach/confidant had begun.

Since then, Jonathon has taught hundreds of clients "purposeful dating" using his proven methods of coaching. Most recently, he has chosen to focus on working primarily with women, who he freely admits tend to be more coach-able than his own gender.

Jonathon Aslay grew up in Redondo Beach, California as part of a quintessential, now increasingly rare, nuclear family. He's a successful entrepreneur and actual graduate of Loyola Marymount University and is blessed with two sons. And, he shares a close relationship with parents who recently celebrated their 63rd wedding anniversary.

Please contact me, Jonathon Aslay, for Private Coaching: JA@UNDERSTANDMENNOW.com or go to my web site: www.JonathonAslay.com

Have you heard about my **Spotlight Coaching Program?** Included you will receive:

* Private FACEBOOK Support Group Page
* Monthly open forum group coaching call (Q&A)
* Monthly workshops / tele classes (Q&A)
* Quarterly Guest interviews (recorded)
* Monthly Newsletter
* Discounts on Private Coaching Sessions
* Raffles for FREE Coaching Sessions
* Plus much more...

TO LEARN MORE click here:
http://UNDERSTANDMENNOW.com/membership

REFERENCES

* *Free Republic Forum*
       <http://www.freepublic.com/focus/fr/611970/posts?page=70>

* *Steele, David- MA, LMFT; "Description of Commitment"*
       <http://www.relatinshipcoachinginstitute.com/role-of-commitment-in-coching-relationships/>

Made in the USA
Monee, IL
08 July 2022

99319334R00077